# Don't Ever Give Up Your Dreams

May your dreams
   never disappear with age,
but may they continue
as alive and as beautiful as you
with the knowledge that they
will someday come true.

— Joanne Domenech

# Don't Ever Give Up Your Dreams

A collection of poems
Edited by Susan Polis Schutz

**Blue Mountain Press** ®

P.O. Box 4549, Boulder, Colorado 80306

Library of Congress Number: 82- 074095
ISBN: 0-88396-183-0

Manufactured in the United States of America
Fifteenth Printing: May 1999

 This book is printed on recycled paper.

The following works have previously appeared in Blue Mountain
Arts publications:

"This life is yours" and "If you know," by Susan Polis Schutz.
Copyright © Continental Publications, 1978. "Love Your Life,"
by Susan Polis Schutz. Copyright © Stephen Schutz and Susan
Polis Schutz, 1982. "I know you're going to make it," by amanda
pierce; "You never know until you try," by Laine Parsons; "Deep
within our hearts," by Edmund O'Neill; "It's natural to feel
disappointed," by amanda pierce; and "There is a funny old saying,"
by Michael Rille. Copyright © Blue Mountain Arts, Inc., 1983.
All rights reserved.

Thanks to the Blue Mountain Arts creative staff.

ACKNOWLEDGMENTS appear on page 62.

**Blue Mountain Press** INC.

P.O. Box 4549, Boulder, Colorado 80306

# CONTENTS

Don't ever give up
your dreams

I know you're going
to make it . . .
It may take time
and hard work
You may become frustrated
and at times you'll feel
like giving up
Sometimes you may even
wonder if it's really
worth it
But I have confidence
in you,
and I know you'll make it,
if you try.

— amanda pierce

You have powers you never dreamed of. You can do things you never thought you could do. There are no limitations in what you can do except the limitations in your own mind as to what you cannot do.

Don't think you cannot.

Think you can.

— Darwin P. Kingsley

Learning isn't easy . . .
frustration tends to set in
    quickly.
You hurt.
You feel defeated.
You want to give up —
    to quit.
You want to walk away
    and pretend it doesn't
            matter.
But you won't,
because you're not a loser —
    you're a fighter . . .

We all have to lose sometimes
    before we can win,
we have to cry sometimes
    before we can smile.
We have to hurt
    before we can be strong.
But if you keep on working
        and believing,
you'll have victory
    in the end.

— Ann Davies

Hold fast to dreams
for if dreams die,
life is a broken
winged bird that
cannot fly.

— Langston Hughes

You never know
until you try.
And you never try
 unless you really try.
You give it your best shot;
you do the best you can.

And if you've done everything
 in your power, and still "fail" —
the truth of the matter is
 that you haven't failed at all.

When you reach for your dreams,
 no matter what they may be,
 you grow from the reaching;
 you learn from the trying;
 you win from the doing.

— Laine Parsons

This life is yours
Take the power
to choose what you want to do
and do it well
Take the power
to love what you want in life
and love it honestly
Take the power
to walk in the forest
and be a part of nature
Take the power
to control your own life
No one else can do it for you
Take the power
        to make your life happy

— Susan Polis Schutz

## In Your Life

There is excitement in your life . . .
be a part of it
There is work in your life . . .
begin with it
There is sorrow in your life . . .
ease the pain away
There is joy in your life . . .
feel it, know it, share it
There are goals in your life . . .
strive for the highest
There is purpose in your life . . .
                    explore it.

                                        — jonivan

I am just beginning
to make some definite changes
    in my life
Some of them will take time,
some will cause me grief,
some will mean risk
and a lot of growing pains, too
But whatever the case,
I know I will make it . . .

It's having someone like you
to see me through
both the good times
and the bad
that makes me so sure . . .

— Gail Nishimoto

The only way to find rainbows
is to look within your heart;
the only way to live fairy tales
is through the imagination and
power of your mind;
the only place to begin a
        search for peace
is within your very soul;
because rainbows,
        fairy tales and peace
are treasures that grow
from the inside out.

— Evelyn K. Tharp

If you have a dream
        alive in your mind,
Bring it to the world, give it life.
Too often, the treasures which are
        ours alone to give
are never given the chance to grow.
We each have a unique gift
        to bring to this world.
It is our purpose in life
        to offer this gift.
For even if only a few people
        benefit from our offering,
the world is then a better place
        to live.

— Susan Staszewski

My Prayer . . .

That I will have the strength
    to carry on,
the patience to try again
    when things go wrong,
the ability to see beauty
    where others see none.
That I will have the hope
    of a new dream
        waiting to be dreamed,
the chance to reach out
and the wisdom to look forward
to tomorrow.

— Donna Wayland

Power
   strength and self assertion
lie within us all
yet we are afraid
we do not use the resources
given to us to lift our lives
from the stagnation of comfortable routine
locked into jobs, relationships . . . ourselves
fearing what others may think of us
we lack the courage to step
      from our accustomed role
strength and self assertion
      can be demonstrated
with gracious kindness
softly spoken truths will take us farther
than belligerent defensiveness
be true to yourself . . . dare to be different
by courageously stepping forward
to say "i am" . . . "i will be"
then "be"
remembering always to move softly
with gentleness and love
free yourself from what others want you to be
that with which you have aligned yourself
find and use the magnificent
loving power within you

— diane westlake

## Love Your Life

We cannot
listen to what
others want us
to do
We must listen
to ourselves
Society
family
friends
mates
do not know what
we must do
Only we know
and only we
can do what is
right for us
So start
right now
You will need to
work very hard . . .

You will need to
overcome many obstacles
You will need to go
against the better
judgment of many people
and you will need to
bypass their prejudices
But you can have
whatever you want
if you
try hard
enough
So start right now and
you will live
a life designed
by you and
for you
and you will
love
your
life

— Susan Polis Schutz

For a happy life . . .

Believe in yourself
   but don't be overconfident;
Be satisfied
   but know that you can always improve;
Accept love graciously
   and always be ready to give more;
Be modest in victory and success
   and courageous in defeat;
Give comfort and security to others
   and you will always receive it in return;
Be glad . . . just for being
   the wonderful person that you are.

— Lee Wilkinson

Set yourself earnestly
to see what you are made to do,
and then set yourself earnestly
to do it . . .
and the loftier your purpose is,
the more sure you will be
to make the world richer
with every enrichment
of yourself.

— Phillips Brooks

Deep within our hearts,
each of us carries the seed
of a secret dream,
special and unique to each individual.
Sometimes another person
can share that dream
and help it grow to fulfillment;
other times, the dream remains
a solitary pursuit, known only
to the seeker. But secret or shared,
no matter what it might be,
a dream is a potential which
should never be discouraged. For
each of us also carries within ourselves
a light which can cause the seed
to grow and blossom into beautiful reality . . .
that same light I've seen shine
so clearly in you.

— Edmund O'Neill

The courage of working for
something you believe in,
day in and day out,
    year after year,
can be difficult
    but holds the greatest rewards.

Find your ideal . . .
        and follow it.

— V. Sukomlin


Be All that You Can Be

Champion the right to be yourself.
Dare to be different
    and to set your own pattern;
Live your own life,
    and follow your own star.

— Lin Yutang

If You Think You Can, You Can

Your mind is your real self —
   your real being.
There are more and more possibilities in nature,
in the elements, in man and out of man;
and they come as fast as man sees
and knows how to use these forces,
in nature and in himself.

Possibilities and miracles
   mean the same thing.

— Prentice Mulford

Today, we share
words and beginnings,
hopes and songs,
expectations for the future —
built from yesterday,
built from now.

Tomorrow . . .
watercolors and rainbows,
impressions and soft scenes,
a tapestry of feelings —
weaved from memories,
weaved from dreams.

— Albert M. Ward

Just as no one can
    tell you how to feel
about a beautiful sunset,
no one can tell you how
    to live your life.
You are the artist . . .
and must shape your
    experiences
with your own hand.

— Susan Staszewski

We grow great by dreams.
Dreamers . . . see things
    in the soft haze of a spring day,
or in the red fire
of a long winter's evening.
Some of us let these great dreams die,
but others nourish and protect them,
nurse them through bad days
till they bring them to
the sunshine and light
which comes always to those
who sincerely hope that
their dreams
will come true.

— Woodrow Wilson

We can do
anything we want to
if we stick to it
long enough.

— Helen Keller

Follow your dreams
and pursue them with courage
for it is the pursuit
of those dreams
that makes life
really worth living.

— Linda DuPuy Moore

living is moving on and up
it is giving in and giving away
the right things at the right time
all it takes is the courage to do it
knowing and believing in the divine timing
of your days
you are new
only when you have released . . .
    totally . . . the old
you must not stay on the same level of being
there always is another way to awareness
grow          change          become
the strength you need deep within
will rise to the surface . . . join consciousness
and bring your transformation
ask for newness
call upon your forces
display your courage
accept the change
believe in your right
to have it


                              — diane westlake

I believe that we cannot live better
than in seeking to become
still better than we are.

— Socrates

Don't waste precious time
worrying about
what you should have done . . .
But rather, focus your attention
on what you are doing now,
and what you want to do
in the future
Don't concentrate
on any mistakes that might
        have been made,
but learn from them.

— Debbie Avery

I dream of beauty
   that transcends time
in a world that knows
   nothing else
Where all is clean and pure
   and good
and all mankind is willing
      to help one another
Where discovery is a way of life
and there is no fear of failure
Where God is a very personal
   thing that is real to everyone
I dream of a time that has
      no pain
and where there is no despair
Where love has a constant
   meaning
that keeps people together
      forever
I dream that all of this could
   someday be true
and I pray that I will share
   it all
      with you.

— Johnnie Rosenauer

Let every day
        be a dream
            we can touch.

Let every day
        be a love
            we can feel.

Let every day
        be a reason
            to live.

— Claudia Adrienne Grandi

A thing
that you
sincerely
believe in
cannot
be wrong.

— D. H. Lawrence


The best of life
is that which
ever reaches upward
and strives toward
better things.

— James R. Miller

If it should happen
that your dreams
are shattered,
do not be afraid.
Have the courage
to pick up the pieces
and smile at the world.
For dreams that are
easily shattered
can just as easily
be rebuilt.

— Chris Jensen

I like you . . .
You feel life way down inside,
You have the courage to think
and the strength to get
  involved.
You are a dreamer . . .
and dreamers are too rare . . .
For few people believe
  enough to dream.

— Linda S. Smith

I wish for you to
be happy,
and to reach
   for the best . . .
for what is happiness,
if not to believe in
and follow
one's dream?

— Theophile Gautier

Find happiness in nature
in the beauty of a mountain
in the serenity of the sea
Find happiness in friendship
in the fun of doing things together
in the sharing and understanding
Find happiness in your family
in the stability of knowing
    that someone cares
in the strength of love and honesty
Find happiness in yourself
in your mind and body
in your values and achievements
Find happiness in
everything
you
do

— Susan Polis Schutz

If you know
who you are and
what you want and
why you want it
and if you have
confidence in yourself and
a strong will to obtain your desires and
a very positive attitude
you can make
your life
yours
if you ask

— Susan Polis Schutz

One day at a time —
this is enough.
Do not look back
and grieve over the past,
for it is gone;
and do not be troubled
about the future,
for it has not yet come.
Live in the present,
and make it so beautiful
that it will be worth
remembering.

— Ida Scott Taylor

It's natural to feel disappointed
        when things don't go your way
It's easy to think . . .
        "I can't do it, so why try?"
But, no matter how scared you are
        of making a mistake
or how discouraged you may become,
Never give up . . .
because if you don't try and
if you don't go after what you
        want in life,
it won't come to you,
and you'll be forced to accept
        things that you know could
            be better . . .

Success is not measured by
        whether you win or
            whether you fail —
there's always a little bit
        of success, even if things
            don't go your way —
What's important is that you'll
        feel better about yourself,
            for the simple reason
                that you tried.

— amanda pierce

Wishing you success . . .

Life is a series of
   beginnings . . .
that bring us closer
to the realization of
   our dreams.

May all of your
   beginnings
be showered by sunbeams
and all of your dreams
   sense the warmth
      of success.

                    — Edith Schaffer Lederberg

A dreamer lives for eternity

— Anonymous

In
your moment of success —
I wish for you
a greater mountain to climb,
a wider sea to sail,
a more profound challenge to meet —
for it has been
the journey to the summit,
the reaching for distant shores,
the tenacity to answer the call
   that has made you
   the most special person you are today.

— Kele Daniels

You are a wonderful,
    worthy and loveable person.
Appreciate that
about yourself.
No one has ever been,
or ever will be,
quite like you.
You are an individual,
    an original,
and all those things that make you
uniquely you
are deserving of love
    and praise.

— Peter A. McWilliams

There is a funny old saying, one that says,
"If you don't ride a bicycle,
you don't fall off!"
What it means to say, of course, is
if you do put a lot of energy into something,
you are bound to make mistakes;
and if you take a lot of risks,
you are bound to tumble here and there.
But remember this: that if you persist,
you will arrive at the destination of your choice.
And if you do occasionally fall in the process,
you'll learn much more than if you don't.

So try, and do, and discover all that you can be.

And take me with you . . .
        in spirit, as you go,
so you'll know that
I'll always be beside you
wishing for nothing but the best.

— Michael Rille

## You Deserve the Best

A person will get only what he or she wants
You must choose your goals carefully
Know what you like
and what you do not like
Be critical about what you can do well
and what you cannot do well
Choose a career or lifestyle that interests you
and work hard to make it a success
Enter a relationship that is worthy of everything
you are physically and mentally
Be honest with people, help them if you can
but don't depend on anyone to make life easy
or happy for you
Only you can do that for yourself
Strive to achieve all that you like
Find happiness in everything you do
Love with your entire being
Make a triumph
of every aspect
of your life

— Susan Polis Schutz

In this special moment in life . . .

Think freely. Practice patience.
Smile often. Savor special moments.
Live God's message. Make new
friends. Rediscover old ones. Tell
those you love that you do. Feel
deeply. Forget trouble. Forgive an
enemy. Hope. Grow. Be crazy. Count
your blessings. Observe miracles.
Make them happen. Discard worry.
Give. Give in. Trust enough to take.
Pick some flowers. Share them. Keep
a promise. Look for rainbows. Gaze
at stars. See beauty everywhere.
Work hard. Be wise. Try to
understand. Take time for people.
Make time for yourself. Laugh
heartily. Spread joy. Take a chance.
Reach out. Let someone in. Try
something new. Slow down. Be soft
sometimes. Believe in yourself. Trust
others. See a sunrise. Listen to rain.
Reminisce. Cry when you need to.
Trust life. Have faith. Enjoy wonder.
Comfort a friend. Have good ideas.
Make some mistakes. Learn from
them. Celebrate life.

— Jan Michelsen

Don't ever give up your dreams . . .
and never leave them behind.
Find them; make them yours,
and all through your life,
cherish them,
    and never let them go.

— Elisa Costanza

# ACKNOWLEDGMENTS

We gratefully acknowledge the permission granted by the following authors, publishers and authors' representatives to reprint poems and excerpts from their publications:

Joanne Domenech for "May your dreams," by Joanne Domenech. Copyright © Joanne Domenech , 1981. All rights reserved. Reprinted by permission.

Ann Davies for "Learning isn't easy . . . ," by Ann Davies. Copyright © Ann Davies, 1983. All rights reserved. Reprinted by permission.

Alfred A. Knopf, Inc. for "Hold fast to dreams," by Langston Hughes. Copyright © 1932 by Alfred A. Knopf, Inc. Renewed. All rights reserved. Reprinted by permission.

jonivan for "In Your Life," by jonivan. Copyright © jonivan, 1983. All rights reserved. Reprinted by permission.

Gail Nishimoto for "I am just beginning," by Gail Nishimoto. Copyright © Gail Nishimoto, 1983. All rights reserved. Reprinted by permission.

Evelyn K. Tharp for "The only way to find rainbows," by Evelyn K. Tharp. Copyright © Evelyn K. Tharp, 1983. All rights reserved. Reprinted by permission.

Susan Staszewski for "If you have a dream" and "Just as no one can," by Susan Staszewski. Copyright © Susan Staszewski, 1983. All rights reserved. Reprinted by permission.

Donna Wayland for "My Prayer . . . ," by Donna Wayland. Copyright © Donna Wayland, 1983. All rights reserved. Reprinted by permission.

Diane Westlake for "power" and "living is moving on and up," by Diane Westlake. Copyright © Diane Westlake, 1980. All rights reserved. Reprinted by permission.

Lee Wilkinson for "For a happy life . . . ," by Lee Wilkinson. Copyright © Lee Wilkinson, 1983. All rights reserved. Reprinted by permission.

Albert M. Ward for "Today, we share," by Albert M. Ward. Copyright © Albert M. Ward, 1983. All rights reserved. Reprinted by permission.

Linda DuPuy Moore for "Follow your dreams," by Linda DuPuy Moore. Copyright © Linda DuPuy Moore, 1983. All rights reserved. Reprinted by permission.

Debbie Avery for "Don't waste precious time," by Debbie Avery. Copyright © Debbie Avery, 1982. All rights reserved. Reprinted by permission.

Johnnie Rosenauer for "I dream of beauty," by Johnnie Rosenauer. Copyright © Johnnie Rosenauer, 1983. All rights reserved. Reprinted by permission.

Claudia Adrienne Grandi for "Let every day," by Claudia Adrienne Grandi. Copyright © Claudia Adrienne Grandi, 1983. All rights reserved. Reprinted by permission.

Chris Jensen for "If it should happen," by Chris Jensen. Copyright © Chris Jensen, 1983. All rights reserved. Reprinted by permission.

Linda S. Smith for "I like you . . . ," by Linda S. Smith. Copyright © Linda S. Smith, 1983. All rights reserved. Reprinted by permission.

Edith Schaffer Lederberg for "Wishing you success . . . ," by Edith Schaffer Lederberg. Copyright © Edith Schaffer Lederberg, 1983. All rights reserved. Reprinted by permission.

Kele Daniels for "In your moment of success," by Kele Daniels. Copyright © Kele Daniels, 1983. All rights reserved. Reprinted by permission.

Peter A. McWilliams for "You are a wonderful," by Peter A. McWilliams. Copyright © Peter A. McWilliams, 1981. All rights reserved. Reprinted by permission.

Jan Michelsen for "In this special moment in life . . . ," by Jan Michelsen. Copyright © Jan Michelsen, 1982. All rights reserved. Reprinted by permission.

Elisa Costanza for "Don't ever give up," by Elisa Costanza. Copyright © Elisa Costanza, 1981. All rights reserved. Reprinted by permission.

A careful effort has been made to trace the ownership of poems used in this anthology in order to obtain permission to reprint copyrighted materials and to give proper credit to the copyright owners.

If any error or omission has occurred, it is completely inadvertent, and we would like to make corrections in future editions provided that written notification is made to the publisher: BLUE MOUNTAIN PRESS, INC., P.O. Box 4549, Boulder, Colorado 80306.